EMBRACING PREGNANCY, YOUR CHILD, AND PARENTING

Your Guide Book to Learn How to Unlock
the Secrets of Successful Parenting

By: Maria Cruz & Patrick Baldwin

Copyright 2017
American Christian Defense Alliance, Inc.
Baltimore, Maryland
ACDAInc.Org

Special Request

Thank you for purchasing our book and supporting our Ministry. We actually have two requests – To Pray for Our Ministry and to Read this Book All the Way through. No Ministry can Survive without Prayers and Support so we ask you to keep our Ministry in Your Daily Prayers and Pray as the Lord leads.

We encourage you to Read the Book you purchased all the way through. Many Books NEVER Get Read, and the ones that do only get read the first few pages.

One of our Special Request is that if you are serious about learning the material in this book that you take time to actually read this book in its entirety – all the way through.

We all lead such busy lives nowadays and can get side tracked so easily, please take a moment to consider my words and read to the end of the book and keep us in Your Prayers.

Thank You once again for purchase. We deeply appreciate Your Prayers and Support and know that God will Bless You as You continue to Bless this Ministry.

Dedication

This book is dedicated to Parents everywhere that embrace their sacred duty to Raise Up their Children in the Way they should Go. You are one of the very foundations of a free and just society - Thank you for all you do.

Forward

Parenting has been described as *"...the absolute best, hardest, heart-felt, gut-wrenching, wonderful, awful, amazing, terrifying, worthwhile thing you will ever do."*

I think that pretty much sums it all up. Parenting is all of those things—sometimes all at the time. But even in the darkest and most difficult moments of parenting your child it is a privilege you wouldn't trade for anything in the world. But why is that?

It is because your children are a part of you—they are bits and pieces of your heart, soul, and mind all squished together to make the unique and wonderful little (or big) person that calls you "Mom" or "Dad". Whether your children are biologically yours or yours through the equally-labor-intensive process of adoption, your children are a part of you and it goes against human nature to not love and cherish a part of ourselves.

That being said, I'm not naïve. I'm a parent, too. I know how hard it is. I know the struggles of wondering if you've made a complete mess of things. I know the feelings of insecurity mixed with overwhelming pride. I know the hope you have for their future and the intensity of the instincts to protect them at all costs and give them everything you possibly can to make their lives as wonderful as possible.

The purpose of this book is to encourage new and soon-to-be-parents to embrace their role with joy and tenacity and to remember that being a parent is the most important job God has given us.

Table of Contents

Chapter 1: Handle With Care

Psalm 127:3 says, *Children are a heritage from the Lord, offspring a reward from Him.*

...from the LORD—that's where our children come from. The LORD. He entrusts them to us to care for; helping them go from infancy to adulthood safely, securely, and in an atmosphere that reflects God's love as much as is humanly possible.

There are a number of verses and passages of scripture in the Bible that reflect and teach this truth. We'll be looking at several of them throughout the pages of this book. I want to begin, however, by taking a look into the heart and mind of the woman I consider to be the most Godly mother of all times. Her name: Hannah.

We are introduced to Hannah in the first chapter of the Old Testament book of First Samuel. Hannah, who is one of Elkanah's two wives, is a tender-hearted and Godly woman who desperately longs to be a mother.

Her inability to conceive a child is something Peninnah, Elkanah's other wife, takes great pleasure in. Peninnah's taunting and ridicule plants seeds of insecurity and doubt in Hannah's mind; doubts that Elkanah quickly puts to rest; assuring his sweet wife that his love for her is true—child or no child.

I'm sure this had to bring at least some degree of comfort to Hannah's heart and mind, but it didn't change the fact that Hannah wanted to be a mom more than anything in the world. Hannah knew, though, that wanting to be a mom wasn't enough. Hannah knew that the gift of motherhood came from one 'place' and one 'place' only—God.

So Hannah prayed. She prayed and she prayed and she prayed some more. But her prayers weren't 'just' to become a mom. Hannah told God that if He would bless her with a child she would give the child back to him—literally.

She told God that if He would bless her with a son she would give him to Eli to be raised up as the next High Priest and Judge over all of Israel.

After praying the prayer Hannah and Elkanah conceived a child. When the baby was born they named him Samuel. And true to her word, when Samuel was about three or four years old Hannah took him to live in the Tabernacle with Eli so that he could learn the duties of the priesthood. Samuel grew up to be a man of deep faith and one who obeyed God to the letter. He was the last Judge of Israel before they demanded that He appoint someone to be their king.

I'm sharing Hannah's story with you to remind you that your children are on loan to you from God. You are their caretakers and their role models. God has charged you with the task, aka, given you the privilege of overseeing some of His most priceless treasures.

As a steward of these treasures you need to be sure you care for them the way God expects you to—the way He told us to in Deuteronomy 6:5-9:

And thou shalt love the Lord thy God with all thine heart, and with all thy soul, and with all thy might. And these words, which I command thee this day, shall be in thine heart: And thou shalt teach them diligently unto thy children, and shalt talk of them when thou sittest in thine house, and when thou walkest by the way, and when thou liest down, and when thou risest up. And thou shalt bind them for a sign upon thine hand, and they shall be as frontlets between thine eyes. And thou shalt write them upon the posts of thy house, and on thy gates.

You are to teach them diligently. When you teach diligently you teach consistently; meaning on a regular basis. But teaching with diligence also implies that you are meticulous and careful to make sure they don't just know *about* God, but that they know who God *is*—His character.

God doesn't just tell us the manner in which we are supposed to teach our children. No, God also gives us the specifics of how to get the job done. He tells us to **talk of them when thou sittest in thine house, and when thou walkest by the way.** He goes on to say we are to teach our children when they lay down and when they are awake. In other words, the Word of God is to permeate our children's lives. Their exposure to God's Word needs to be the norm—not the exception. We are to **teach our children to see God** in everything, **give thanks** to God for all things, **give God the credit** He is due, and **give God total control** of our lives.

And then He gets to the really personal part. Teaching our children these things needs to be done by example. Children really do learn what they live, and God is calling us to make sure they live in homes where God is first and foremost every day and in every way.

That's a pretty tall order—an awesome responsibility. It is not impossible, though, because God never gives you a job to do without also providing you with the resources necessary to do it…and do it well.

The Word of God …prayer…the Holy Spirit…Godly counsel from other parents…a parent-heart that wants to give their children the best life possible—these are the resources we have at our disposal.

You need to know, however, that these resources aren't meant to be optional. Deuteronomy 6 isn't a suggestion or a wish. It is a command from the creator to the moms and dads He entrusts with His most priceless treasures.

Hannah knew she was raising Samuel *for* God. Raising your children *for* God is your job, too.

Chapter 2: The Miracle of Life

Have you ever looked at a newborn baby? I mean really looked—their tiny fingernails, the perfect little curvatures of their ears, the soft little eyelashes, the way they instinctively know when Mom is nearby? They are pure perfection, aren't they? They are also a living, breathing miracle.

Yes, life is a miracle. It couldn't just happen by accident. Too many things have to be just right in order for an egg and sperm to get together and stay that way. Oh, I know there are those first-time-I-had-sex-I-got-pregnant people out there. But they are far from the norm. In fact, the UK's Daily Mail website and the New York Post newspaper reported that research conducted on three thousand couples showed that on average, it takes couples one hundred and four sessions of lovemaking before pregnancy is achieved.

Additional research shows that less than half of all couples get pregnant within the first six months of trying to conceive, but that just over ninety percent conceive within a year. So like I said, there's nothing accidental or coincidental about it.

I also know that getting the news that you are expecting can take you on a rollercoaster of emotions. Excitement, disbelief, anxiousness, fear, awe, surprise, elation…and sometimes disappointment and anger are the most common.

Not every pregnancy is planned or desired. Most teenagers aren't trying to achieve pregnancy when they're in the back seat of a car or home alone on the couch. Sometimes couples don't feel ready to start a family for one reason or another, but find out they are anyway. Other couples feel their families are complete and/or are getting ready to be empty-nesters when suddenly….

For others—especially couples who have experienced the grief of miscarriage or infertility—pregnancies can be scary. They want it so badly they are too afraid to let themselves enjoy it. They don't want to get their hopes up only to have their hearts broken again.

And then there are those that count down the days from the time their chances of conceiving were the highest until they can take a pregnancy test to see if this will be the month.

No matter what you are feeling or thinking, though, you need to know that God knows exactly what's going on and he knows exactly what He is doing. He knew wayyyyyyyyy back when he said, "Let there be light…" when each of us would be conceived. I know that's a lot to wrap your head around, but it's true.

The Bible says so in Psalm 139:15-16:

My frame was not hidden from You, When I was made in secret, And skillfully wrought in the lowest parts of the earth. Your eyes saw my substance, being yet unformed. And in Your book they all were written, The days fashioned for me, When as yet there were none of them. (NKJV)

Every mother out there can testify that giving birth and being a parent is truly a gift from God – The Miracle of Life if you would. Hopefully God will see fit in His plan to bless you abundantly with children in the near future. Just remember Children have angels assigned to watch over them so make sure you're gracious to strangers.

Hebrews 13:2 says, "Do not forget to show hospitality to strangers, for by so doing some people have shown hospitality to angels without knowing it."

As far as I know I've never welcomed an actual angel into my home, but I have been the recipient of their God-given ability to intervene in my life in a way that still leaves me 'on my knees thankful'.

Remember: Babies aren't made by accident. A mommy and daddy's perfect timing doesn't even guarantee anything. It is God's perfect timing that results in the miracle of life.

Chapter 3: Meant to be Parents

Genesis 1:27-28 says, *"So God created man in His own image; in the image of God He created him; male and female He created them. Then God blessed them, and God said to them, "Be fruitful and multiply; fill the earth and subdue it; have dominion over the fish of the sea, over the birds of the air, and over every living thing that moves on the earth."thing that moveth upon the earth."*

Genesis 9:1 says, *"So God blessed Noah and his sons, and said to them: "Be fruitful and multiply, and fill the earth."*

In Genesis 28:3, Isaac said to Jacob, *"May God Almighty bless you, And make you fruitful and multiply you, That you may be an assembly of peoples;*

And finally, Psalm 127:3-5 tells us, *"Lo, children are an heritage of the Lord: and the fruit of the womb is his reward. As arrows are in the hand of a mighty man; so are children of the youth. Happy is the man that hath his quiver full of them: they shall not be ashamed, but they shall speak with the enemies in the gate."*

It isn't difficult to see the common thread running through these four verses, is it?

God wants us to be parents. Next to worshipping Him and sharing the message of the Gospel to anyone and everyone we possibly can, being a parent is the most important job God gives us to do. Remember: the job of parent is synonymous with being the caretaker of God's most precious and priceless treasures…children.

Unfortunately, not every parent knows just how important their job is. If they did, the National Children's Alliance wouldn't have to report that over 700,000 children in the US are treated or receive some type of service because of abuse or neglect each and every year. Additionally, over 3 million children in this country are the subject of an intervention or protection order.

Why do you think this is? Why would anyone want to harm an innocent child? The answers to that question are varied. Some would say it is because the parents were abused or neglected, so they don't know any better. Others would say it is because these parents is not mature enough to be a parents. And still others would say that an abusive parent's actions are beyond their control because of an addiction or emotional/mental disorder. While these things may or may not be true, the real reason child abuse/neglect happen is because God is not present in the home.

When God is absent from a home a lot of other things are absent, as well. Things like patience, gentleness, genuine selflessness, diligent teaching about God, and unconditional love.

As Christians we need to be conscientious about making sure God is present in our homes. We have the same perspective on parenting that God designed us to have. We need to make sure we embrace our role as parents; viewing it as a praiseworthy responsibility rather than a chore. It is a praiseworthy responsibility we need to take to heart.

Some would ask then, if being a parent is something God desires us to do, then why are there Christian couples suffering from infertility? And if being fruitful and multiplying is so important, then where does that leave couples who don't want children or those who don't marry? Are they living outside of God's will for mankind?

Infertility is an emotionally and physically painful condition. But know this…infertility is NOT a sin and it is NOT God's way of punishing someone. Infertility is a medical condition caused by a number of different things. What's more, infertility doesn't mean you cannot be a parent. Adoption is always as possibility. The process isn't always easy and (take it from someone who knows) it is considerably more labor-intensive than having a biological child. And don't let anyone ever tell you that adoptive parents aren't parents in every sense of the word, because they are.

Choosing to be childless is not a sin, either. Christian couples choose to remain childless in order to be able to pursue their ministries without the distractions of family. Frank and Ella are an example of this mindset.

Frank and Ella spent thirty years as dedicated youth directors. Neither felt comfortable or working with small children or babies.

Tweens and teens, however, were a different story. They poured themselves into ministering to young people this age and their efforts were highly effective. So rather than having biological children of their own, this couple chose to 'have' dozens of children over the years; loving, teaching, and mentoring them to know and love the LORD. Other couples may choose not to have children for any number of reasons that are personal in nature; reasons that are between them and the LORD. For anyone to pass judgement on these people would be very wrong.

According to scripture God prefers we have children. Children are proof of the love between a man and a woman. Children are the hope of the future—both the future of this world and of the Church. So be fruitful and multiply; raising your children to know the LORD and that they are fearfully and wonderfully made by Him and for Him.

Chapter 4: We're Having a Baby

You've been anxiously waiting for the days and weeks to pass so that you could take a pregnancy test. The day came, you took the test, and you are on 'cloud nine' because the test came back positive. YOU ARE GOING TO HAVE A BABY!

In the days immediately following, you and your spouse shared the good news with family and close friends. You've pinched yourself (literally or figuratively speaking) a few times to remind yourself you aren't dreaming—that this is actually happening. You and your spouse have already started tossing a few names around and you have already had your first mini-panic-attack over whether or not you can go through the labor process and then actually be responsible for a helpless baby. If so, relax. All of these thoughts (and a whole lot more we're getting ready to talk about) are completely normal.

They are just part of the whole pregnancy experience. Your thoughts and worries are no different than those of any other parent-to-be, so we're going to spend the next few minutes talking about the most common thoughts and concerns of parents during those first few days and weeks following the moment you find out that you are going to have a baby.

Telling your spouse

It wasn't all that long ago women didn't have the capability to find out whether or not they were pregnant until they were at least eight weeks into the pregnancy or without going to the doctor to have blood drawn to test to see if the level of the hormone, hCG is high; indicating there is a pregnancy.

It also wasn't all that long ago expectant fathers weren't nearly as involved in the pregnancy experience or the birth of their baby as most expectant fathers are today.

Expectant fathers were usually unaware pregnancy was even a possibility until their wife shares the good news.

Today things are a lot quicker, easier, and a lot more of a joint effort. The prospective parents communicate a lot more directly about the possibility of whether or not pregnancy is possible. If, however, you are an expectant mom who wants to surprise your husband with the wonderful news, there are a number of fun ways to do so.

Give your husband a baby onesie with the logo of his favorite sports team, and a note that says 'from' your baby saying can't wait to meet you Dad, a giant cookie with your approximate due-date written in icing, or a devotional book for dads - nice.

Telling your family and close friends

Your parents, grandparents, and siblings should hear the news before the general public does.

A phone call or face-to-face visit to share your good news may be a bit 'plain', but it gets the job done. If you want to spice it up a bit try gifting grandparents with a t-shirt or mug with a grandparent saying on it is always fun. Phone calls, emails, or posts on your social media are effective and sufficient for telling friends and extended family members about your pregnancy.

Telling your employer

A close friend of mine had to go to her new boss the second day she was on the job and tell him she was pregnant. The pregnancy was something she and her husband had all but given up on happening, so learning she was going to be a mother again was an answered prayer. But it was also nerve racking. She didn't know her new employer so she had no idea how he would take the news. Thankfully he was gracious and understanding and did not treat her any differently than he did any other employee.

Telling your employer should be a priority. They need to know so that you can discuss how things like prenatal appointments and maternity leave are handled. You also need to talk to the HR person to find out what your insurance does and does not cover—what your options are regarding participating providers.

While there are some jobs that might require you to go to a limited duty status or make some special arrangements for bouts of morning sickness, being on your feet too long, or other such things. You need to remember that being pregnant is not a disease or a disability. Don't treat it as such by taking advantage of your coworkers or employer.

Choosing an OBGYN

More than likely you already have a doctor who will care for you throughout your pregnancy and who will deliver your baby. You have probably been seeing them for your yearly exams. But there are instances in which this is not the case. If for example you have to move for a job just prior to giving birth – you will need to find a new doctor.

The whole doctor situation can be a bit unnerving. You want someone you can trust, right? Someone you feel comfortable with. Because this isn't always possible it is just one more reason for you to put your faith in the Great Physician—Jesus. He is always on-call. He will never be too busy to care for you. He knows your every need and those of your baby. He is the one you can always put your trust in and know He's got your back.

Early good prenatal care is essential

No matter who your doctor is or how and when you tell everyone else about the baby growing inside of you, the most important thing you can do for yourself and your baby is to take great care of yourself physically and emotionally.

Thankfully, most expectant moms don't have any trouble tweaking their normal lifestyle or routines once they find out they are expecting. You know—things like giving up caffeine, bouncing over rough and rocky trails on an ATV, or even putting their hobby of refinishing antique furniture on hold.

I'm here to suggest, however, that you start these things before you know you are pregnant. If you are trying to get pregnant you want to create the most welcoming, healthy, and conducive environment for your growing baby as possible.

So if you are reading this book in anticipation of the day you find out you are pregnant, start making those changes today. If you are newly-pregnant there is no question that the things I mentioned above (along with several others) are no-no's for pregnant women wanting a healthy pregnancy and healthy baby. But if there are somethings you are in question about, don't hesitate to ask your doctor.

Congratulations! This is a wonderful, special, and amazing time in your life. Enjoy it. Make it among the happiest months of your life.

Chapter 5: The First Trimester

This book combines the biological and physiological aspects of pregnancy with the spiritual aspects of pregnancy. So in addition to learning or being reminded of what is taking place inside you (or your wife) I am also going to provide you with Scriptures of encouragement and reminders that your baby is a treasure in God's storehouse of treasures, and in spite of all that He created, He sees each and every single one of us as priceless... irreplaceable...one-of-a-kind.

Fertilization

"Do you know the time when the wild mountain goats bear young? Or can you mark when the deer gives birth? Can you number the months that they fulfill? Or do you know the time when they bear young? ~Job 39:1-2

In spite of the fact that you may be planning to try to become pregnant by charting your ovulation times, the fact remains that there is only One who knows the moment fertilization takes place and a new life begins. That One is God.

Within those first few hours when the egg and sperm join together, a new life is formed that contains chromosomes from each parent. These chromosomes determine the sex of the baby along with a host of other things – but those things I'm sure you may already know about so let's move on . . .

The earliest stages of formation

For You formed my inward parts; You covered me in my mother's womb.
~Psalm 139:13

Looking at a picture of a three week-old baby may not provide a very clear picture of what is going on inside, but wonderful things are happening.

By the end of the third week after conception, your baby's body is basically three layers of cells that are working hard to form various intricate parts of the body. The first layer of cells forms the skin, the body's nervous system, and their eyes and ears. The second layer is what grows to become the baby's heart (along with the rest of the circulatory system), their bones, muscles, and ligaments, their kidneys, and their reproductive system. The inner-most layer of cells forms the respiratory and digestive organs and systems.

A brain, spine, arms, and legs

I will praise You, for I am fearfully and wonderfully made, Marvelous are Your works, And that my soul knows very well.
~Psalm 139:14

Four weeks after your baby has been conceived, which is usually around the time most women find out they are pregnant, they are starting to develop a brain, the spinal column is forming, and arms and legs look like little buds ready to sprout to be fully infant-sized.

Your baby is growing and developing their most important parts for living a healthy, well-rounded life. This is just another reason you need to make sure you are taking proper care of yourself so that your baby receives the best of care, too.

Accepting the Child God Gives You

For the body is not one member, but many. If the foot shall say, because I am not the hand, I am not of the body; is it therefore not of the body? And if the ear shall say, Because I am not the eye, I am not of the body; is it therefore not of the body? If the whole body were an eye, where were the hearing? If the whole were hearing, where were the smelling? But now hath God set the members every one of them in the body, as it hath pleased him. ~1 Corinthians 12:14-18

Weeks five and six following conception are busy ones, to say the least. The shape of the head becomes more distinctive, as do the eyes, ears, and nose. While your baby cannot yet see, the retinas are forming; meaning and it won't be long before they can.

Fingers begin to form on the little short arms that are still yet to grow to their full length. The upper lip is formed, and the neck becomes straighter and more distinguishable.

Most amazingly of all (in my opinion, anyway) is the fact that all of this is happening to a little person about the size of a penny!

During the final weeks of the first trimester your baby's size goes from that of a penny to about the size of a credit card.

By the time the first trimester comes to an end your baby also has toes, elbows, definite eyelids, buds inside the mouth that will eventually become baby teeth, red blood cells are being produced by the liver (yes, that's there, too), and their genitalia begins to make its presence known on the outside of the body.

No wonder you don't feel like your normal self

Now if God so clothes the grass of the field, which today is, and tomorrow is thrown into the oven, will He not much more clothe you, O you of little faith? "Therefore do not worry, saying, 'What shall we eat?' or 'What shall we drink?' or 'What shall we wear?' For after all these things the Gentiles seek. For your heavenly Father knows that you need all these things..
~Matthew 6:30-32

Now that you've been given a very brief and basic rundown of what is going on inside a woman's body during those first weeks of pregnancy, do you even have to ask why they don't feel like themselves? Is it any wonder that extreme fatigue is completely normal for expectant mothers, as is nausea, aka morning sickness?

These first weeks and months can be physically and emotionally exhausting. There's no doubt about that. But as a Christian you have the promise that God can and will sustain you through this time so that you can enjoy the blessings of being a steward of one of His treasures.

Chapter 6: The Second Trimester

As you enter into the second trimester of your pregnancy, you usually begin to feel better (no more morning sickness) and your energy level begins to rise. For many women, the second trimester of pregnancy is a time when they feel better than they've ever felt. They are excited about the baby's upcoming arrival. They are enjoying the fact that they are growing a baby-bump; bringing with it all sorts of positive attention and well-wishes. Thinking about names, nursery décor, and all the other fun things that go with becoming parents seem to start taking root during the second trimester.

While everything going on, on the outside is great, what's happening on the inside is even more thrilling. Let's take a look…

Diapers not needed...yet

As you do not know what is the way of the wind, Or how the bones grow in the womb of her who is with child, So you do not know the works of God who makes everything..
~Ecclesiastes 11:5

Beginning around the eleventh week after conception (which is technically the thirteenth week of pregnancy because the two weeks between ovulation and what would have been your next period are counted) your baby begins to pee. Their pee becomes part of the amniotic fluid your baby will live in until they makes their grand appearance into the world.

Along with that major developmental milestone, your baby's bones are hardening, more red blood cells are forming in other organs, and their sex organs are becoming more distinctive.

Something new almost every day

Before I formed thee in the belly I knew thee; and before thou camest forth out of the womb I sanctified thee, and I ordained thee a prophet unto the nations. ~Jeremiah 1:5

As you progress further into your second trimester your baby starts developing more and more of the functions and characteristics they will need to live outside the womb. They develop the ability to hear, blink their eyes, and their heart is pumping around one hundred pints of blood each day. Your baby is also rolling and flipping around quite a bit, but is still too small for you to feel these movements. Don't worry, it won't be long before you do. Additionally, their digestive system is now working and they are almost as long as a dollar bill.

Reaching the halfway mark

But the very hairs of your head are all numbered. ~Matthew 10:30

During the second trimester you will hit the half-way mark of your pregnancy. It is about this time that an ultrasound can reveal to you the sex of your child (if you want to know).

Being able to recognize your baby as either a boy or a girl isn't the only significant milestone in your baby's development during this time though. Throughout the remaining weeks of the second trimester of your pregnancy you will begin to feel your baby's movements. This is one of the most exciting aspects of pregnancy. To be able to feel your baby moving around inside your body is…is…well, there really are no adequate words to fully capture the specialness of how this feels (physically or emotionally).

It is also possible for the baby's father, grandparents, or whoever else you invite, to feel the baby's movements by placing your hand on your tummy during the baby's more active times. This, too, is a very special event and a precious bonding experience for husbands and wives and for soon-to-be-dads and their unborn child.

Discovering the sex of your baby and being able to feel their movements isn't the only things that happen during these final weeks of the second trimester. There are also many significant things going on inside your baby's body.

The sound of your voice

My son, hear the instruction of thy father, and forsake not the law of thy mother: For they shall be an ornament of grace unto thy head, and chains about thy neck .~Proverbs 1:8-9

Your baby has definite times of being asleep and awake. They can even be awakened by your movements and noises outside the womb. I find this incredible, don't you!

Your baby's body is covered in the cheesy coating and a fine layer of fuzz or hair. These things both serve to keep your baby's skin from being chapped by the amniotic fluid.

Your baby's fingerprints and footprints are engraved onto their little bodies. Each one, we know, different from anyone else's every born.

Your baby can suck their thumb and recognize Mom's voice. Yes, that's right— *they know your voice before they ever see your face!*

By the end of the second trimester your baby's lungs are developing at a rapid pace; preparing them to make their grand entrance in a few months.

But because the baby's lungs and their ability to suck properly are not yet fully established, it is important that you take care to keep your baby from making their entrance too soon to avoid complications. If that happens, however, just remember God is the One in Control and He has a plan for everyone including your baby.

By the time you come to the end of your second trimester your baby weighs approximately two pounds and is approximately nine inches long – and that to me is just Awesome to think about.

Chapter 7: The Third Trimester

You're almost there—'there' being the end of your pregnancy. At this point you are feeling both excited and nervous. You are getting tired of wearing maternity clothes, yet are 'certain' you'll never be able to wear anything a 'normal' woman wears again. You have days you feel energized and ready to take on the world, but then others you feel like a beached whale that can barely get one foot in front of the other. It's that whole rollercoaster effect kicking into high gear again.

This is also the point in your pregnancy when you begin getting serious about preparing the nursery, enjoy putting all those tiny little clothes in the closet and dresser drawers, and preparing for maternity leave from your job.

At this point you also need to be finalizing arrangements for childcare once you return to work—if you plan to do so. I cannot stress how important this is, because the weeks you are home with your baby after he or she arrives fly by all too quickly. In other words, you aren't going to have the time or desire to deal with this issue while on maternity leave, so it is essential you do so now.

I also want to tell you how important it is to *enjoy* these last few weeks of your pregnancy. These are special weeks in your life—weeks that cannot be replicated no matter how many children you have. Each pregnancy story is different and needs to be experienced as the miracle it truly is.

Getting ready, but not quite set to go

For we are his workmanship, created in Christ Jesus unto good works, which God hath before ordained that we should walk in them. ~Ephesians 2:10

The third and final trimester of your pregnancy is your baby's time to develop and grow into all those finishing touches that make us capable of living outside the womb. During these last few weeks your baby's hair comes in on their heads or not(it just depends on your family).

Your baby is also stretching and kicking— sometimes causing you a good deal of discomfort. For example, one mom delivered her second daughter with an extremely bruised tailbone—bruised from the inside due to the baby's near-constant kicking and jabbing –ouch! And then there are those more comical incidents surrounding the baby's movement during the last trimester. More than one expectant mom I know has had a bowl of popcorn or other snack resting on her belly, only to have it knocked off by the baby's movements.

Your baby can and will likely have hiccups; something you can feel them doing, but cannot help them with.

At the onset of the third trimester your baby will also start working quite diligently to put on weight. The added weight and layers of fat they form fill out their skin making it less wrinkled and protects their hardening bones. This protection is necessary, because even though their bones are hardening, they are still quite soft in comparison to what they will be later on. Remember—they have to be pliable enough to make it through the birth canal.

The Father's finishing touches

The spirit of God hath made me, and the breath of the Almighty hath given me life.
~Job 33:4

Thirty weeks after conception (week thirty-two of your 'official' pregnancy) your baby starts breathing practice. They are gearing up for the outside world. To this point they have breathed in and out, but it has been more instinctive than purposeful.

At this point in time the bulk of the fuzz that has covered your baby's body also begins to fall off. The degree to which this happens varies greatly in each child. As you may already know, some babies are more hairy than others when they are born. Premature babies are especially so, if born before this stage of development. The amount of baby fuzz isn't an indicator of anything being wrong with the baby. It is simply just one aspect of their unique nature showing through.

In the final weeks of gestation your baby develops the ability to detect light. They gain about an ounce of weight per day, the added weight and fat content causes their little bodies to fill out even more, and they begin positioning themselves into the birth canal.

Your doctor will likely be checking you weekly at this point to make sure everything is going as it should.

Some doctors even do an ultrasound toward the end of the pregnancy to check to make sure the umbilical cord isn't wrapped around the baby's neck, to make sure the baby's head is not so large that they feel it would be unsafe for the mother to have a vaginal delivery, and a number of other things.

It is also at this point that mothers who are having a c-section will schedule their baby's delivery. Most c-sections are scheduled to take place the week of the due date or possibly a few days prior to the due date the mother was given. This is done in an effort to avoid the baby trying to come on its own, which in most cases of mothers having C-sections, would not be a good thing.

Most C-sections are done for the sake of either the mother or child's physical condition. However, if at all possible I strongly recommend having a vaginal birth as there are many added health benefits for the baby.

Remember, the last stages of your baby's development are important to you and to them. So continue to take care of yourself and to give your baby every possible opportunity to grow and develop the way God intended them too.

Your third trimester (and pregnancy) is almost over. D-day is fast approaching.

Chapter 8: Let's Do This

At this point in your pregnancy you probably have the crib set up, you've been to childbirth classes (if you chose to take them), you have your bag packed for the hospital, and a solid birthing plan in place. You know exactly how you want things to go and you have every intention of making the birth of your child an absolutely, positively, perfectly wonderful experience.

The only thing you aren't counting on is the fact that more often than not, the best laid birthing plans fly right out the window about the time the contractions start coming around five minutes apart.

This really hurts

To the woman He said: "I will greatly multiply your sorrow and your conception; In pain you shall bring forth children; Your desire shall be for your husband, And he shall rule over you." ~Genesis 3:16

With the first baby you 'know' it's going to hurt. You've talked to other moms. You've read a few books and watched a few movies. But geez, how hard can it really be? If it was *that* bad there wouldn't be as many babies as there are. If it was *that* bad, not even sex would make it worth the 'risk'.

The thing to remember is that every women is different and every birth is different. When my wife started getting contractions I thought it was false labor and went back to sleep because I had exams the following day. However, shortly thereafter she came back in, woke me up, and said "It's Time to Go". We contacted the OBGYN and got everything we needed and headed out.

When she got to the hospital she was close to 5cm dilated. My wife no doubt is a solider and not every women could handle that as if it was no big deal but there are some.

Keep in mind my wife is just over 5' tall and weighs a little over 100lbs (not including the pregnancy weight). So if she can do it you probably can too. Just don't have any preconceived ideas about how much pain it will be because you truly don't know.

The experience of giving birth is not something you can plan for right down to your baby's first cry. There are too many variables you have no control over. Things like: where you are when your labor starts, how long the labor and delivery will take, how cooperative your baby is, how well you work with your body's natural instincts to get the job done, and the overall type of labor experience you have.

If you are reading this and think that because you are about to give birth to baby number two, don't get too smug. Every birth is different. Don't believe me? Ask any mom who has more than one child.

That thing they say about the pain being worth it...they're right

A woman, when she is in labor, has sorrow because her hour has come; but as soon as she has given birth to the child, she no longer remembers the anguish, for joy that a human being has been born into the world.
~John 16:21

I'm not going to spend a lot of time talking about the actual labor and delivery process or about the things that take place within the first few hours and days following your child's birth. Your doctor will cover all of that, and that's as it should be.

What I do want to say is that becoming a parent truly is a cause for joy and celebration. It really is the most amazing and most important thing you will ever do in this world—second only to giving your life to Christ.

So will you really forget the pain? Will the memory really go away?

The Word of God is true in all ways—
including this. Though you will remember
that it hurts and your memories of the event
will always be there, the memories will be
such that you will see the marvelous good
that came from it—not the anguish and
suffering you felt.

Chapter 9: Family

Welcoming a new baby into your family is news parents don't hesitate to share while having a big smile plastered across their face and heart. Think about it…how many birth announcements have you gotten that say something like, "We're as happy as we can be to announce we are now a family of three!" or "Our family is growing day by day now that baby number three has come to stay."?

Parents, grandparents, aunts, uncles, cousins should all be a part of your child's life for so many reasons. There are far too many to cover them all adequately, lets take a few minutes to cover the most important ones now…

Family provides a sense of belonging

God set up the institution of family because He knows we thrive best when we have the communion of relationships. He knows we need to be needed and need to be wanted. He knows family units and provides the sense of belonging He created us to want and need.

Family brings a sense of responsibility

Having a child changes you—or at least it should. Having a child causes you to be less selfish and more selfless. You suddenly find yourself completely and utterly responsible for another human life. You realize that what you do and how you do it affects someone else. You realize that where you go, how you act, what you say, and everything else about your life isn't just about you—it's about you and your baby.

Family becomes more important

How many new parents have you heard say something to the effect that when their baby was born their own parents (the baby's grandparents) suddenly became wiser and smarter than they'd ever been before?

News flash! The grandparents didn't suddenly become anything (other than grandparents). The wisdom and knowledge was there before the baby was born. But when faced with the awesome and daunting task of actually being a parent themselves, well....

The role of grandparent, aunt or uncle can be a precious resource in the lives of children and their parents.

For a child, these extended family members can be sounding boards, people who have time when parents don't, an added source of encouragement and unconditional love, someone to teach them skills their parents don't have, someone to just hang out with, someone to whom they can give back all of these things, and someone they can look up to as an example of faith.

Those of you who have families that can bring these things into your child's life should be thankful for the blessing of family. It is something you should not take for granted and should not deprive your child of.

Those of you who do not have family to lean on and glean from, do not have to miss out completely. You can 'adopt' a family in your church. There are undoubtedly people as hungry for a family as you are. Family isn't always about blood and DNA. It's about exhibiting the kind of love that says "I love you just because".

Never forget those that claim the name of Jesus Christ and claim His Blood are Adopted into the Family of God – So You are NEVER Alone!.

Chapter 10: Children are the Future

Babies and children just add that something extra into a family's dynamics. They bring a sense of innocence, wonder, fun, and youthfulness into a home. Children also give us purpose—or at least they should. Being a parent should make you stand a little taller on the 'ladder' of integrity. They should make you think on your words before you speak them; making sure they are honest, kind, and fair. Children should make you walk a straighter path; working hard, spending your money wisely, being honest and forthright, and setting a solid example of how to live. Children should make you desire to know God more fully and to teach them to know God on a personal level, too, because children are the future of society and of the Church.

One of the most heart-rending statements I've ever heard went something like this: The worst possible feeling a parent could have is the feeling that they might not spend eternity with their children in heaven.

Ouch! That cuts deep, doesn't it? As parents we need to be mindful of the fact that we are responsible for raising our children to know the LORD and to have a desire to seek his purpose for their lives.

That being said, you need to remember that your purpose is to raise them to know these things—not live their lives for them.

We have this Promise from God . . . .

Train up a child in the way he should go, And when he is old he will not depart from it. ~Proverbs 22:6

While none of us are perfect; meaning we all make parenting mistakes (and plenty of them), if we do our job to raise our children as directed by God in the Bible, we have nothing to worry about. You can do it as God fearing Parents that seek the Living God and honor Him by following the Word of God on how to raise your children.

Don't let things discourage or frighten you, along the way. There will always be ups and downs in life but in all things God is an ever present help in a time of need – Trust in Him, Allow His Word to inspire you to become a great parent who raises awesome kids.

Do as we are told in Lamentations 2:19…

Arise, cry out in the night: in the beginning of the watches pour out thine heart like water before the face of the Lord: lift up thy hands toward him for the life of thy young children that faint for hunger in the top of every street.

In reading this book you have either learned or have been reminded of the fact that being a parent isn't just something physical that you do. Being a parent is also a spiritual act—one that God intends to be a spiritual act of worship aimed at Him.

God knows that when we see our children as the priceless treasures they are we will love, nurture, and cherish them in such a way that glorifies God.

Special Gift

God has a Gift for You!   The Plan of
Salvation:

There is no formal prayer of salvation as
many churches would have you believe,
God's Word is very clear - there is only one
way to get to the Father in heaven and that is
through Jesus Christ (John 14:6). Jesus says
that you must be born again to enter into
heaven (John 3:3-5).

Salvation is simply the first step in building
an open and honest relationship with God.
We all have sinned and fallen short, but
there is Hope in Jesus Christ - Just cry out to
God in sincerity and honesty asking for
forgiveness and for Him to Save you,
Sanctify you, and fill you with His Holy
Spirit - Ask for His will to be done in your
life on earth as it is in Heaven and That's it,
now just keep it real with God.

A Warning:

The Christian walk is not an easy life on the surface. The Word of God says that we will be hated in all the world for Christ namesake (Matt. 24:9). The Bible says that in the last days are enemy prevail against us physically until Christ returns to save us (Dan 7:21, 22). Furthermore, we must endure hardship as a good soldier of Jesus Christ (2 Tim 2:3) and yet we are never alone in this, God promises us that He will never leave us nor forsake us if we believe in him (Matt.28:20).

In everything we go through we have the peace and joy of God which surpasses all understanding (Philp. 4:6-8) The Bible declares, "For I consider the sufferings of this present time are not worthy to be compared with the glory which shall be revealed in us". (Rom 8:18). However, in all these things we are more than conquerors through Jesus Christ (Rom. 8:37)

Stay In Contact

Our Contact Information

Stay in Contact with the American Christian Defense Alliance, Inc. through Our Website At: ACDAInc.Org

Join Our Mailing List

We also Greatly Appreciate You Signing Up For Our Mailing List and Providing a Good Rating and review for this Book. Your reviews help other people like yourself find this book on Amazon and benefit from its contents.

If You or Your Family have been Blessed by this book please let us know by dropping us a line through our website at ACDAInc.Org

Find All Our Books

A Vague Notion: How To Overcome
Limiting Beliefs of Fear and Anxiety
Through the Word of God

Parenting Special Needs Children: A
Christian Guide to Parenting Children with
ADHD, Autism, Asperger's, and other
Psychological, Behavioral, or Physiological
Disorders

Race Relations in America: A Christian
Guide to Help Unite Christians in the Faith

Martial Arts Ministry: How To Start A
Martial Arts Ministry

Biblical Bug Out: Don't Bug In - Follow
The Calling

Christian Prepping 101: How To Start
Prepping

How to Finance Your Full-Time RV Dream

Additional Platforms

Thank you for reading this book. Your support and the support of others continue to enable our Ministry to grow. We hope and pray that this book has blessed you. If you enjoyed this book consider purchasing it on additional platforms or giving it as a gift to someone who could benefit from it.

We have this book available as an E-Book, Paperback, and Audio Book. We have no way to know which platform you purchased our book on but want to make you aware of another way you can help support our Ministry if you haven't yet listen to the audio book version of this book.

If you Enjoy Listening to Audio Books in General Consider Signing Up For Audible.com. If You've Been On the Fence About Signing Up for Audible.com or Would Just like to Support Our Ministry By Purchasing Our Audio Book First – We Would Greatly Appreciate It.

Did You Know that You Can Support Our Ministry By Listening to Our Audio Books on Audible.com?

Here's How:

- Sign Up as a New Aubdible.com Member

- Purchase Our Audio Book First and

- Stay an Audible.com Member for at least 61 Days

If You Follow these Simple Steps Our Ministry will Earn $25.00 -$50.00 Every Time This Process in Completed. The Amount we earn is based on if we have narrated the book ourselves or outsourced it to another narrator.

We Greatly Appreciate Your Support as Well as You Sharing this information, including links to our books on Audible.com with Others on Your Social Media Platforms

Thank You Once Again for Your Support; We Know God Will Bless You as You Have Blessed This Ministry

WHOLE COUNSEL

| THE PUBLIC AND PRIVATE |
| MINISTRIES OF THE WORD |

Essays in Honor of Jay E. Adams

DONN R. ARMS AND DAVE SWAVELY, EDITORS

Institute for Nouthetic Studies, a ministry of Mid-America Baptist Theological Seminary, 2095 Appling Road, Memphis, TN 38016 mabts.edu / nouthetic.org / INSBookstore.com

Whole Counsel, The Public and Private Ministries of the Word: Essays in Honor of Jay E. Adams
by Donn R Arms and Dave Swavely, eds.

Copyright © 2020 by the Institute for Nouthetic Studies.
ISBN: 978-1-949737-85-1 (Print)
ISBN: 978-1-949737-86-8 (eBook)
Editor: Donn R. Arms
Design: James Wendorf | www.FaithfulLifePublishers.com

Library of Congress Cataloging-in-Publication Data
Names: Arms, Donn R. and Dave Swavely, eds.
Title: *Whole Counsel, The Public and Private Ministries of the Word*
Description: Memphis: Institute for Nouthetic Studies, 2020

Identifiers: ISBN 978-1-949737-85-1 (paper)
Classification: DDC 230'.42

Published in the United States of America